MEDIUM HIGH

C000133378

ITALIAN ART SONGS of the ROMANTIC ERA

Edited by Patricia Adkins Chiti

Phonetic transcriptions by John Glenn Paton

LAY-FLAT BINDING

ABOUT THIS EDITION

Alfred has made every effort to make this book not only attractive but more useful and long-lasting as well. Usually, large books do not lie flat or stay open on the music rack. In addition, the pages (which are glued together) tend to break away from the spine after repeated use.

In this edition, pages are sewn together in multiples of 16. This special process allows the book to stay open for ease in playing and prevents pages from falling out. We hope this unique binding will give you added pleasure and additional use.

Copyright © MCMXCIV Alfred Publishing Co., Inc.
All rights reserved. Printed in USA.

Cover art: *Florence, Duomo from the Mozzi Garden, 1877*
by Henry Roderick Newman
Watercolor and bodycolor on paper (9 7/8 x 13 3/4 in.)
Virginia Steele Scott Collection, Henry E. Huntington Library and
Art Gallery, San Marino.

ISBN 0-7390-0245-7 (Book)
ISBN 0-7390-0246-5 (Book and CD)

TABLE OF CONTENTS

PREFACE

This volume brings to light some of the best songs that were written in Italy in the 19th century, songs that were widely popular in their time. Included here are composers of world fame and others who have been forgotten for decades, but all of them were highly respected during their lifetimes. Only a few opera composers have survived the changing waves of fashion, but there is much to be learned and enjoyed in rediscovering the songs and the composers represented here.

These songs were written during the period of rising Italian national feeling known as *il Risorgimento* (the resurgence). In 1871 the Papal States surrendered to secular authority, and Rome was chosen as the capital of a nearly unified Italy (complete unification took place during World War I). Until that time what we know as modern Italy was in fact a series of kingdoms, dukedoms, republics and church governed states, each with its own form of society and cultural traditions.

Morlacchi, Rossini and Vaccai were born within the Papal States, where greater importance was given to liturgical and sacred music than to the *opere liriche* (operas) so popular in the rest of the peninsula. Mercadante, De Giosa and d'Arienzo were born to the south in the Kingdom of the Two Sicilies. Catalani and Senekè came from the Grand Duchy of Tuscany. Donizetti, Ponchielli and Ferrari were born to the north in the realms of Lombardy and Venetia.

Almost every city had an opera house running a successful season where new works and past triumphs were programmed by enterprising impresarios. Notwithstanding the social and political upheavals during *il Risorgimento*, there continued to be a constant demand for new works. As wealthy bourgeois families followed the lead of the aristocracy in establishing regular musical evenings and salons, there was a greater demand for printed sheet music that was suitable for home use. This need was met by a rapidly expanding music publishing business.

In 1807 the publishing firm of Artaria in Milan brought out the first sheet music printed by the so-called "new method," which was developed in Rome in 1805 by dell'Armi for the preparation of maps and illustrations. Artaria later sold the patent to Ricordi. The major publishing

This 1827 engraving was made from a portrait of Gioacchino Rossini. He was richly dressed, as befitted the possessor of two national titles: *Composer to the King* and *Inspector General of Singing in France*. At the time of this portrait, he was about 35 years old and his operatic reputation was still rising; no one suspected that he would soon stop composing operas altogether. Another 20 years passed before he composed "La Separazione," the song in this volume.

Places Named in the Text

houses of Ricordi, Lucca and Sonzogno in Milan and Cottrau and Girard in Naples initially prepared and sold reductions of the most popular operas for voice and piano. These were followed by isolated arias and then by songs for voice and piano, *romanze da camera*, especially commissioned by the publishers. Such songs quickly became the most widely sold form of sheet music. They were used for study purposes, sung in private homes, and later sung during public soirées arranged by newly formed con-

cert societies. In the second half of the century *romanze* reached an even larger public through the pages of a number of important monthly and bimonthly music magazines. Printed by the music publishers themselves, music magazines gave news about the opera houses and concert venues, along with the latest theatrical, social and musical gossip. Each issue also contained a new work for piano or for voice and piano.

Naturally enough, given the enormous number of pieces written and

This engraving of Nicola Vaccai was the frontispiece to the biography written by Vaccai's son Giulio (*Vita di Nicola Vaccai*, Bologna: Zanichelli, 1882).

printed, one must search among them to identify the pieces that are particularly original and are of the highest level of musical quality. This vocal literature has rarely been studied seriously by music historians because many have believed, erroneously, that the art songs of the period were only popular songs in a more bourgeois form.

Songs written for voice and piano early in the 19th century were very similar in style to the arias that could be heard in any opera. The first song in this volume was designated as an *aria* by its composer. The songs composed by Morlacchi, Vaccai and Rossini tended to be written to poems in an "Arcadian" style, one which portrays a rustic life of idealized emotions. The melodic lines and embellishments of such songs were identical to those used in operatic arias. Often these are designated as *arie, ariette,* or *scene*, even though they do not appear in any opera.

By far the most common name for an art song in the 1800s was *romanza* (romance). Publishers often added the designation *da camera* (for the room), emphasizing that this music is not for the church or theater, but rather for the home or concert hall.

Melodia, although used to express melodic vocal phrases in Italian music from Monteverdi's time onwards, also appears as a designation of an art song. From around 1830 Hector Berlioz and other French composers, such as Pauline Viardot-Garcia, used the term *mélodie* for their songs. The Italian composers who used the term *melodia* were for the greater part those who visited France, worked there, or had constant contact with French culture, such as Rossini, Donizetti and Ferrari.

Many *romanze* incorporate folk rhythms and dance forms, such as the *barcarola, tarantella* and the Florentine *stornello*. In 1829 the Neapolitan composer and publisher Guillaume Cottrau wrote to his sister explaining that he wanted to put together an album of songs based on his own collection of local melodies:

> "I should like to include works from all over Italy, and I have already written to [composer Simone] Mayr to have some of Donizetti's Venetian, Bolognese and Romagnole songs."

The local folk songs and street songs were reinvented completely, even though traditional harmonies and rhythms could still be heard in *ballate* (ballads), *canzoni* (short songs with many stanzas), and *nennie* (Sicilian style dirges).

The most common form of *romanza*, however, is the song which tells a story or describes a particular emotional state: great joy, sorrow, hope, despair, motherhood, national pride, etc. The heroes and heroines of these songs are often the innocent victims of a tragic personal or historical destiny, for instance, Rossini's

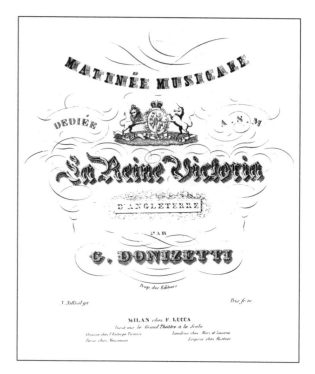

La Separazione or Mercadante's *L'Abbandonata*. Another protagonist of these songs is often a figure living at the edge of society: an orphan, a mistress, a gypsy (d'Arienzo's *La Zingara*), or a knight errant (Ponchielli's *L'Eco*).

The choice of these subjects should not lead us to believe that the composers were in any way interested in writing songs with social statements; the texts chosen were similar in every way to the popular literature of the period. Italians loved romantic tragedies, historic and gothic novels, and sentimental stories.

Toward the end of the century, with the arrival of a form of operatic drama called *verismo* (realism), an extended aria, which often appeared to be an elongated melodic recitative and therefore more "realistic," found its way into the drawing room. Composers of this school called their songs *liriche* (lyrics), since they were freer in form than the *romanze* of the earlier decades. And so while more traditional composers like d'Arienzo and Senekè wrote *ballate* and *romanze*, Ponchielli and Catalani composed the more forward-looking *liriche*.

The all-important relationship between text and music found in the German *Lied* is not nearly so vital to the Italian *romanza*. Occasionally one finds settings of poetry by great classical authors such as Dante Alighieri, Manzoni or Leopardi, or of new texts by well known opera librettists such as Count Pepoli, Felice Romani, or Marco d'Arienzo, but many of the poets remain unnamed.

Only six songs in this book have texts by poets whose names are well known, but more frequently one has the impression that the composers used whatever text was set before them, and quite often wrote their own. Carlotta Ferrari, herself a writer with a passionate interest in politics, set songs to texts by Jacopo Vittorelli, and Alfredo Catalani, a German literature enthusiast, composed songs to poems by Heinrich Heine.

Some mention should be made here of the special importance of the city of Naples for this book. Most of our composers either were born in Naples or studied there, or furthered their own careers by writing operas for the demanding and critical Neapolitan public. From the time of Alessandro Scarlatti Naples was an important operatic center. The so-called Neapolitan School consisted of generations of musicians who were trained in one or another of the conservatories of Naples.

There is even a distinctive harmony that is named after Naples, the Neapolitan Sixth chord, the first inversion of a major chord which is built on a lowered second degree of a minor scale. Some Neapolitan folk melodies have the lowered second scale degree, and the Neapolitan Sixth chord is heard in several of the songs in this book, for example, in Mercadante's *La Stella* at measure 53.

CHARACTERISTICS OF *ROMANZE*

*R*omanze are at their best when the piano accompaniment underlines the melodic line with simplicity, sobriety, clarity and a vein of Mediterranean melancholy. Many composers used the piano instead as a sort of alternative for a full orchestra, writing pages of arpeggios, repeated chords, threatening tremolos, dramatic pauses, sudden fortissimos. All of these devices could be found in any operatic score, but they are of questionable effectiveness or taste when transferred to the piano. Occasionally the composer alternates recitatives with short arias, as in Mercadante's *La Stella* and Senekè's *S'io t'amo*, and these particularly theatrical songs contain more elaborate embellishments, cadenzas and dramatic changes in tone color and dynamics. However, most *romanze* have relatively simple piano accompaniments because their authors knew that they would be played by amateur pianists.

Songs were commissioned and written with a definite public in mind. Italian girls from wealthy families studied singing in the same way they studied the piano, the harp or the mandoline, or etching and fine needlework. *Romanze* allowed them to display their prowess at family and society gatherings. But with the advent of the music magazines with their song inserts, *romanze* reached a much larger public throughout Italy. Magazines and single songs were bought by people of every social class and condition, by professional and tradespeople, in the cities, the provincial towns and even in the country. Furthermore, by the second half of the 1800s upright pianos could be found in homes everywhere.

Italian composers in the 18th and 19th centuries were trained to sing, to play the piano and violin, to compose and orchestrate, and, above all, to write operas. These were written for a public that loved to sing. The success of an opera was judged by whether the opera-goer could sing the tunes while leaving the theater. In addition, the easy flow of the Italian language, the naturally well placed vowels, which encourage a good legato line and florid ornamentation, and the singable consonants have made the Italian language one of the easiest, if not *the* easiest, to sing.

Songs were originally dedicated to wealthy students or important patrons, but toward the end of the 1800s many songs were dedicated to famous singers, in the hope of being included in their concert programs, or to society hosts and hostesses. Such dedications to the rich and famous served as a sort of advertisement to increase the sale of the songs, much in the same way as the rich and famous today lend their names and faces to sell commercial products.

INTERPRETING ROMANZE

How should *romanze da camera* be performed? They are *not* operatic arias and were not composed for performance in opera houses or for large modern concert halls. They were written to be heard in ballrooms, large drawing rooms, small public concert halls, or private homes. Dramatic songs may be performed in an exciting way but should not become unduly melodramatic. Sentimental songs may be sung with pathos but not with realistic sobs or sighs.

One should first read the text to understand the general mood of the song. Is it telling a story or is it describing an emotion or is it a nonsense song? Next, one should look at the vocal line and see whether this is long and flowing with an even tessitura or whether it consists of large intervals, leaps, or staccato notes. Is it divided between recitative and aria sections? Lastly, one should look carefully at the piano part to see what sort of harmonic background has been given to the melodic line. Measures of arpeggios written beneath an ample and calm melodic line mean that whatever the text is about, the general atmosphere must be calm and tranquil. It is important to remember that the indications given at the beginnings of the songs—*andante, allegro, con spirito, agitato*—are not only indications of the tempo of a piece, but also of its spirit.

Where a portion of a song is in recitative style, one must take care to enunciate the recitative clearly, almost as if one were speaking the words. Where a song is *scherzoso* (joking), great attention must be paid to staccato notes, the lengths of phrases, and the crispness of the explosive consonants.

Authentic *bel canto* singing requires clean legato lines and perfect equality of color and tone. Slurs, exaggerated consonants, and high notes held unduly long are out of place in this music. *Portamenti* from one note to another are to be avoided unless the composer has clearly marked them with a slur sign in the score. (More is said below about portamentos.)

Most *romanze* can be sung by either women or men, provided the text is not too emphatically either female or male in point of view. Traditionally, songs written for a female narrator would not be sung by a male voice (e.g., *La Volubile*). It is more often acceptable for male-oriented songs to be sung by a female voice.

In the Italian language there is no neuter, no "it." All words are either feminine or masculine, and I have left the gender of each song as originally written. Some of the songs can be sung by both men and women with a few word changes, and where this is the case I have given alternatives.

VOCAL ORNAMENTATION

I n the 17th and 18th centuries composers expected singers to ornament their arias, even to improvise variations during performances. Certain appoggiaturas were customary and a trill was expected before every final cadence; Italian composers seldom wrote these obligatory ornaments into the score.

In the 19th century composers took more control: From Rossini onwards, composers carefully wrote the notes they wanted, used symbols to indicate the desired ornament, and discouraged interpreters from inserting their own embellishments. As a result, Italian music of this period appears to contain a great many ornaments, but there actually may be fewer ornaments than singers of

previous generations would have sung on their own initiative. In any case, it will not be found necessary to add ornamentation to any of the songs in this book, as one would do in arias of the 17th and 18th centuries.

Composers did, however, expect every singer to understand the conventional written symbols for *appoggiature, acciaccature, gruppetti* and *portamenti*, as well as the conventional style of performing recitatives.

As early as 1817, Anna Maria Pellegrini Celone had written *Grammatica, ossia regole per ben cantare* (Grammar, or rules for singing well), setting out the use of embellishments, and this was followed in 1826 by Pietro Lichtenthal's *Dizionario e Bibliografia della Musica*, where the use of each ornament is carefully explained and illustrated. Nicola Vaccai's *Metodo pratico di canto italiano per camera* (Practical method of Italian singing for the chamber) arrived on the scene in 1834; it includes carefully formulated exercises which teach the correct performance for each ornament. (A modern edition of Vaccai was prepared by John Glenn Paton for G. Schirmer, Inc., in 1975.)

Before describing the various ornaments individually, some general points should be emphasized. Ornaments are not meant to be difficult but to be expressive. The conventional ornaments of Italian singing probably had their origin as artistic representations of the effects that strong emotions have on the voice.

This portrait of de Giosa appeared in the operatic news journal *Teatro Illustrato* in May 1882, when he was 46 years old.

This portrait of Ponchielli appeared in the operatic news journal *Teatro Illustrato* in April of 1881, when he was 46 years old.

The *appoggiatura* (to be found in songs 1, 2 and 7) is a leaning note or grace note carrying the accent; it takes at least half the value of the note that follows it (or at least one third of the value of a dotted note). It is sung on the beat and has a definite rhythmic value.

The *acciaccatura* (to be found in songs 5–7, 9, 10, 12 and 13), sometimes referred to as an *appoggiatura breve* (a short leaning note), is a short grace note intended to be sung as quickly as possible. It must be thought of as being sung before the beat on which the following note occurs. No interpretation is written out in this book because the slight amount of time needed is indefinable.

The *gruppetto* (to be found in songs 2 and 3), called a "turn" in English, is sometimes indicated by the sign ∾ and sometimes written out in full in small notes. Rossini used both methods. A turn usually consists of a principal note, the next note above, the principal note

again, and then the note below, followed again by the principal note, all of which are performed in quick, equal succession. However, a turn may be sung in different speeds, depending on the emotional content of the song or phrase where it occurs.

The *portamento*, which is found in songs 3–9 and 11–14 and also occurs as a *delayed portamento* in song 3, is one of the most common embellishments found in music of the period. *Portamento* or *portando la voce* literally means "carrying the voice," that is, taking the voice up or down from one pitch to the next. It is an effect obtained by gliding with the voice, without changing vowels, from one note to another lightly and quickly. Lichtenthal stated that the portamento was the opposite to "staccato singing, and one should pass with legato sound from one note to another, with perfect equality of sound whether one is singing an ascending portamento or a descending one."

Del resto bisogno distinguere il buon portamento di voce dal così detto strascinar la voce, simile allo sdrucciolamento del dito sopra uno stromento di corda.

Furthermore, one must distinguish a good portamento from the so-called dragging the voice, similar to the sliding of the finger on a stringed instrument.

Teresina Brambilla Ponchielli is pictured here in the April 1884 edition of *Teatro Illustrato*. The Brambilla family, who lived in Cassano d'Adda near Milan, included five sisters who were all operatic singers. Their niece Teresina was a prominent dramatic soprano who created many of the leading roles in Ponchielli's operas, and later became his wife. She performed many leading roles in Verdi operas with the composer conducting.

Vaccai also said this about the portamento:

Per portare la voce non devesi intendere che si debba strascinare da una nota all'altra, come abusivamente si suol fare; ma unire perfettamente un suono coll'altro, ... anticipando quasi insensibilmente colla stessa vocale della sillaba precedente la nota che segue . . . .

To carry the voice does not mean that one ought to drag from one note to another, as is done offensively, but to unite perfectly one sound with another, . . . almost imperceptibly anticipating the note that follows with the vowel of the preceding syllable . . . .

Some portamentos include a change between two syllables and are shown by a slur marking. Others are done on one syllable; because the two pitches would be connected with a slur anyway a verbal instruction is necessary, either *con portamento* or *portando la voce*. If singers sometimes treat a normal slur as a portamento, this is a matter of taste.

Written portamentos, those marked with a slur between two syllables, occur in the 11 songs cited previously. Mercadante was especially fond of portamentos, using many of them in each song.

Vaccai described a second kind of *portamento*:

L'altro modo, meno usato, è posticipando quasi insensibilmente la nota, e pronunciandone la sillaba con quella che si lascia . . .

The other way, less used, is delaying the note almost imperceptibly and pronouncing its syllable on the pitch of the note that is being left . . .

Rossini provided examples of this "delayed portamento" in his song, measures 14 and 16.

The *mordente*, found in song 2, is an ornament consisting of a principal note, a neighboring tone, and the principal note again. A mordent may be written out using either the upper or the lower neighboring tone.

Double grace notes, in Italian called *appoggiature doppie* or *appoggiature aspirate*, were first introduced into Italian singing by Gasparo Pacchierotti (1740–1821), a famous castrato soprano and an important singing teacher. His embellishment was later used by many composers; it is found in songs 3, 5, 6 and 14. Double grace notes appear to be similar to the *mordenti*, but they are sung on the same syllable as the following note and are closely tied to it, which invariably means that they must be performed earlier than seems necessary on paper.

Cadenze, found in songs 3, 6, 11 and 13, are brilliant passages introduced towards the conclusion of a song or part of an aria. In the Baroque period arias or songs very often concluded with a long trill on the next to last note, and this grew into a much longer freely sung passage where the singer was allowed to show off her or his voice to its fullest advantage. However, by Rossini's time many composers felt that singers were exaggerating with their cadenzas and so preferred, as the songs in this book clearly demonstrate, to write out the cadenzas they wanted. (The singer is not invited to introduce more cadenzas or to substitute others for the songs in this book.) The tempo used for the performance of a cadenza is usually much slower than the tempo of the rest of the song, and the performer has a great deal of freedom of interpretation.

Maria Malibran (1808-1836) was a soprano whose brilliant career was tragically cut short when she was killed by a fall from her horse. She is shown here as Desdemona in Rossini's *Otello*.

ABOUT THIS EDITION

Every song in this book is reproduced from the earliest edition that could be found, usually the first edition. Most of them come from my personal collection; some have been photocopied in major libraries.

Unhappily, even though printing techniques had greatly improved by the mid-19th century, many errors slipped through the printer's net. Such errors have been corrected without special comment. Spelling has been modernized, and punctuation has been supplied where it was missing.

I have added occasional suggestions for dynamics and expression; these are printed in gray to distinguish them from the composers' original markings. Suggestions for breathing have been given using two different conventional signs, *wedges* and *commas*. Wedges are used when breath must be taken to clarify the phrasing or the dramatic content of the song, while commas indicate that a breath is optional.

Current practice is to use slur marks to indicate melismas, that is, to connect with a slur all notes that are sung on the same syllable. Any other slurs in this book are slurs that were placed by the composer. A slur that connects two notes on different syllables is to be understood as a *portamento*, as described elsewhere. Longer slurs that connect several syllables indicate the composer's wish for an especially expressive legato.

Acknowledgments

I should like to thank John Glenn Paton for his invitation to prepare this book and his constant help once I had put things together. Also to be thanked is Dr. Suzanne Summerville, who brought us together.

My special thanks must go to my husband, Gian Paolo Chiti, who has encouraged me to continue to research and collect wonderful music of the past, and to Dr. Domenico Carbone, Director of the Library at the Conservatorio di Santa Cecilia, Rome, for his help and interest in my work.

The only thing left to say at this point is the very Italian *Buona fortuna e buon divertimento!*—Lots of luck, and enjoy yourself singing these songs!

Patricia Adkins Chiti
Rome, Italy

This title page of "La Separazione" contains the dedication "Composed for his student, Mrs. Corinna de Luigi." The first edition of this song was published in two keys.

HO SPARSE TANTE LAGRIME

Francesco Morlacchi
frantʃesko morlakːki
(Perugia, 1784–Innsbruck, 1841)

ɔ   sparse ta̠nte   la̠grime
1 Ho   sparse tante   lagrime
I-have shed   so-many tears

per amːmolːli̠rtil   kɔr
2 Per ammollirti   il   cor,
to   soften-of-you the heart,

ke sta̠ŋko son   di pja̠ndʒere
3 Che stanco son   di piangere;
that tired   I-am of weeping;

ti laʃːoʃ al   tu̠o rigo̠r
4 Ti lascio al   tuo rigor.
you I-leave to-the your harshness.

se aspɛtːti lu̠ltime o̠re
5 Se aspetti l'ultime ore,
If you-await the-last hours

ɛ ta̠rdi   la   pjeta̠
6 È tardi   la   pietà....
is too-late the pity,

ke   pasːsa in no̠i lamo̠re
7 Ché   passa in noi l'amore,
because passes in us love

si ko̠me in no̠i leta̠
8 Sì, come in noi l'età....
yes, as   in us age.

Background

Francesco Morlacchi studied music in his hometown, then for a time with the composer Nicola Antonio Zingarelli (1752-1837). He then studied further in Bologna, where he knew the somewhat younger Rossini. The success of his early operas in Rome and Milan led to an invitation to Dresden, capital of the kingdom of Saxony, now in Germany. In 1811 he received an appointment for life as chief conductor of the Royal Chapel and director of the Italian Opera. In Dresden he commissioned and produced many new Italian operas and went to great lengths to compete successfully with the rival German Opera, which was directed by the composer Carl Maria von Weber (1786–1826).

Morlacchi was a friend and colleague to Spontini, Salieri, Meyerbeer and Bellini. His most popular opera, *Il Barbiere di Siviglia*, was written in 1816, the same year as Rossini's rather better known opera with the same title.

It is not known when Morlacchi composed this *"aria,"* but it appeared in print for the first time in the bimonthly music magazine *La Musica Popolare* (first year, number five), 1882, published by Sonzogno, Milan. This magazine would later become known as *Teatro Illustrato* and would give news about Italian opera houses and, of course, theatrical and social gossip.

"Ho sparse tante lagrime" is typical of Morlacchi's production, and it might well have been composed for a talented student. He chose to interpret the rather sad text in agitated terms: the singer has lost patience after many attempts to please someone who remains hard-hearted. This anger motivates a display of vocal agility, seconded by brilliant passages in the piano.

The second stanza of the text, beginning *"Se aspetti...,"* receives three contrasting treatments: *cantabile* (measures 39–58), then more slowly and thoughtfully (58–64), then more brilliantly, with scales that illustrate how quickly time and love can fly. Both the text and the music of the first stanza return, slightly varied and extended.

Some observations about diction are in order. When a word ends in *i* and the following word begins also with an *i*, as in *ammollirti il cor*, the two vowels should be sung as one.

The *r* at the end of a word preceding another word that begins with a vowel, as in *per ammollirti*, should be flicked, not rolled, whereas the *r* before the *t* in *ammollirti* should be rolled.

When an *e* is combined in a diphthong with an *o* or an *a*, as in *ultime ore*, care should be taken to join the vowels but to enunciate them clearly one after the other. In this particular case, one must sing the *e* very quickly, passing on to the *o*, which is sustained. It is also possible to modernize and simplify the words, singing *ultim'ore*.

The adjective *stanco* indicates that the poet is male, but the song is obviously intended for a female singer. It has always been quite acceptable in Italian music for women to sing male-oriented words, both on and off the operatic stage.

Ho sparse tante lagrime

Aria

Francesco Morlacchi

Literal translation: I have shed so many tears trying to soften your heart, that I'm tired of crying; I'll leave you on your own.

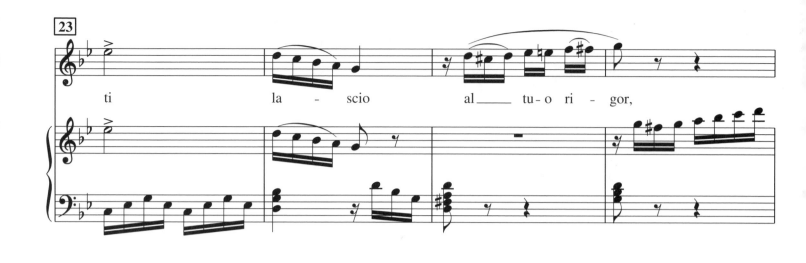

ti la - scio al___ tu - o ri - gor,

ti la - scio al___ tu - o ri - gor!

Se a -

He who waits until the last minute finds that it's too late to have any sympathy. Love can pass us by, in the same way that the years pass by.

sì,   co - me in noi l'e - tà,

8va

sì,   co - me in noi l'e - tà.

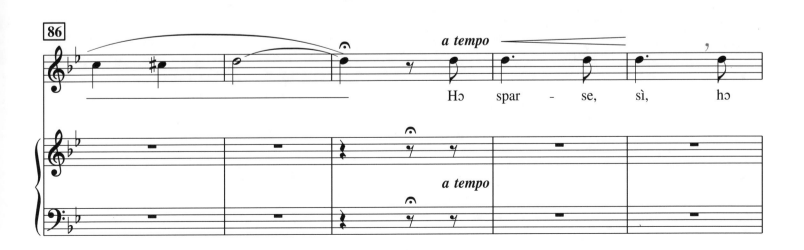

a tempo

Ho spar - se, sì, ho

a tempo

L'ADDIO

[lad:di̱o]

Nicola Vaccai
[niko̱la vak:ka̱i]
(Tolentino, 1790–Pesaro, 1848)

ad:di̱o   dora̱ti so̱n:ɲi
1 Addio,   dorati   sogni,
Farewell, golden dreams,

ka̱ri fanta̱zmi ad:di̱o
2 Cari fantasmi, addio!
dear spirits, farewell.

rit∫ɛt:to nel   ko̱r   mi̱o
3 Ricetto nel   cor   mio
Shelter in-the heart mine

pju   non avɛ̱te
4 Più   non avete.
more not you-have.

bo̱ski soli̱ŋgi e   val:li
5 Boschi solinghi e   valli,
Woods lonely and valleys,

e   po̱d:ʒi e kwɛ̱to ri̱o
6 E   poggi e queto rio
and knolls and quiet river,

ad:di̱o   per sɛmpre ad:di̱o
7 Addio   per sempre, addio.
Farewell for always, farewell.

pju mjɛ̱i non sjɛ̱te   no
8 Più miei non siete,   no.
More mine not you-are, no.

le   stɛ̱l:le ed il silɛntsjo
9 Le   stelle ed il silenzio
The stars and the silence

di no̱t:te or   non voʎ:ʎi̱o
10 Di notte or   non vogl'io.
of night now not want-I.

ad:di̱o   mjɛi dʒo̱je ad:di̱o
11 Addio,   miei gioie, addio.
Farewell, my joys, farewell.

fug:go la pat∫e ad:di̱o
12 Fuggo la pace. Addio!
I-flee the peace. Farewell.

a̱i   nel rumo̱r del   mo̱ndo
13 Ahi, nel rumor del   mondo,
Alas, in-the uproar of-the world

il   dwo̱l non tro̱va ob:bli̱o
14 Il   duol non trova obblio.
the sorrow not finds forgetting.

la mo̱rte ɛ il so̱lo ad:di̱o
15 La morte è il solo addio,
The death is the only farewell

ko̱ra   mi pja̱t∫e la mo̱rte
16 Ch'ora   mi piace, la morte!
which-now me pleases, the death.

Background

Nicola Vaccai received a diploma in music from the Accademia di Santa Cecilia in Rome and went on to study operatic composition with Giovanni Paisiello (1740-1816) in Naples.

Vaccai's most successful opera was *Giulietta e Romeo* (1825). When the famous mezzo-soprano Maria Malibran (1808-1836) sang the role of Romeo in Bellini's *I Capuleti e i Montecchi*, she insisted on singing Vaccai's final scene instead of Bellini's. After Malibran's tragic death in a riding accident, Vaccai, together with Donizetti, Mercadante and others wrote a funeral cantata in her honor.

Vaccai was destined to leave his name in music history not as a composer of operas but rather as a singing teacher. Rossini said: "He had a profound knowledge of the physiology of the human voice and was able to keep his students within their natural limits, thanks to a method which allowed them, at the same time, to sing in the most natural and heartfelt manner."

Singing and teaching in London in 1830-33, Vaccai published his *Practical Method of Italian Singing*, still used by voice students everywhere. He also composed at least 36 *romanze*.

"L'Addio," written for Vaccai's student Luigia Branca, appeared for the first time in Ricordi's magazine, *Glissons n'appuyons pas*, Dec. 3, 1836. The first two stanzas of the poem together form the first part of the aria, which moves from the minor key to the relative major. The final words, *"Addio, addio,"* make an abrupt transition back to minor.

The second part of the aria has some interesting variations in the vocal line; it ends as the first one did, with an abrupt return to minor.

Vaccai's *Practical Method* demonstrates the precise rhythmic notation of appoggiaturas (although the note values are distorted in all modern editions except that of G. Schirmer, Inc.). Following Vaccai's examples, the appoggiatura in measure 10 completely replaces the note of resolution; the dissonance is resolved on the second beat of the measure, not before. Also, the appoggiaturas in measures 37 and 41 replace the succeeding notes.

The custom of using an appoggiatura to notate a dissonance went out of style during Vaccai's career; later composers were more specific about their wishes.

L'Addio

Romanza

Nicola Vaccai

Poco agitato

Ad - dio, do - ra - ti

so - gni, ca - ri fan - ta - smi, ad - di - o! Ri -

cet - to nel cor mi - o, più non a - ve - te, più _____ non a -

a To be performed:

ve - te, più _____ non a - ve - te. Ad -

Literal translation: Farewell, golden dreams; dear spirits, farewell. There is no room for you in my heart anymore.

Lonely woods and valleys, hills and quiet streams, farewell forever. You are no longer mine.

© To be performed:

gl'i - o.   Ad -

I crave the stars and the silence of the night no longer.

Farewell, all joys. I fly from peace. Woe is me, in the strife of the world sorrow cannot be forgotten.
Death is the only true farewell;

the only farewell is death, which pleases me.

LA SEPARAZIONE (The Separation)

[la sepaɾatsjo̱ne]

Gioacchino Rossini
[dʒoakːki̱no rosːsi̱ni]
(Pesaro, 1792 - Passy, near Paris, 1868)

mu̱to rima̱ze   il   labːbro
1 **Muto   rimase   il   labbro**
Mute   remained   the   lip (mouth)

il   di   ke   ti   perde̱i
2 **Il   dì   che   ti   perdei,**
the   day   that   you   I-lost,

ma   de̱ʎːʎi   afːfe̱tːti   mje̱i
3 **Ma   degli   affetti   miei**
but   of-the   affections   mine

non   si   kambjɔ   la   fe
4 **Non   si   cambiò   la   fé.**
not   itself   changed   the   faithfulness.

spaɾi̱ro   i   soɲːɲi   lje̱ti
5 **Spariro   i   sogni   lieti,**
Vanished   the   dreams   happy;

pa̱rver   torme̱nti   lo̱re
6 **Parver   tormenti   l'ore**
seemed   torments   the-hours

kwa̱ndo   lafːfli̱tːto   kɔ̱re
7 **Quando   l'afflitto   core**
when   the-afflicted   heart

si   sovːve̱nia   di   te
8 **Si   sovvenìa   di   te.**
itself   reminded   of   you.

tenta̱i   leni̱r   la   pe̱na
9 **Tentai   lenir   la   pena,**
I-tried   to-allay   the   pain,

e   da̱ltro   amo̱r   fu̱i   va̱go
10 **E   d'altro   amor   fui   vago,**
and   of-other   love   I-was   desirous,

ma   la   tu̱a   bɛlːla   imːma̱go
11 **Ma   la   tua   bella   immago**
but   the   your   beautiful   image

ovu̱ŋkwe   mi   segwi̱
12 **Ovunque   mi   seguì.**
everywhere   me   followed.

a   si   per   te   mi̱o   bɛ̱ne
12b **Ah   sì!   Per   te,   mio   bene,**
Ah,   yes!   For   you,   my   dear,

laʃːʃa̱i   la   pa̱trja   tɛrːra
13 **Lascai   la   patria   terra,**
I-left   the   homeland   soil

ke   un   mɛ̱sto   sol   riskja̱ra
14 **Che   un   mesto   sol   rischiara:**
which   a   sad   sun   lights

fo̱rse   lonta̱no   o   ka̱ra
15 **Forse   lontano,   o   cara,**
Perhaps   far-away,   o   dear-one,

non   sofːfriɾɔ̱   kozi   nɔ   nɔ
16 **Non   soffrirò   così.   No,   no.**
not   I-shall-suffer   thus.   No,   no.

Background

Gioacchino Rossini was the son of a part-time horn player and a professional singer. His career as an opera composer is well documented and, as is well known, he wrote his last opera, *Guillaume Tell*, for the Paris Opéra in 1829. From that time onward, except for his *Stabat Mater* (1841) and *Petite Messe Solennelle* (1863), Rossini wrote only smaller works: piano music; vocal studies, exercises and cadenzas; and many *ariette* and *romanze*.

"*La Separazione*," set to a text by a certain Dr. Fabio Uccelli, was described by Rossini as a *melodia drammatica*. Composed in 1857 for his student, Corinna de Luigi, it was first published by Escudier, Paris, and later by Ricordi, Milan.

Rossini has clearly indicated every nuance-- color, tempo change, accent, ornament-- that is to be used in performance. He continually tried to persuade singers to perform only what he had put on paper, and not what they wanted to "invent." These are some of the technical devices demanded in this song: measure 6, *gruppetto* or turn, accent; measure 9, *portamento*; measure 14, *portamento* with postponement; measures 43 and 44, different kinds of articulation within slurs. The wedge-like accents give a heavier emphasis to the notes, the dots a lighter sound. All of these refinements are within the framework of a highly dramatic delivery. The piece ends with a cadenza written to show off the color and equality of the voice from top to bottom.

The text of the song is in four four-line stanzas, with the addition of a few words (line 12b above) that Rossini added for the sake of a musical transition.

As in the first song in this book, the text has a male orientation but was intended for a woman to sing. If a woman is uncomfortable with this, she needs to change the gender of only two words: *vago* to *vaga*; and *cara* to *caro*.

Spariro is a contracted form of *sparirono. Parver* is a contraction of *parvero.*

La Separazione

Melodia drammatica

Fabio Uccelli

Gioacchino Rossini

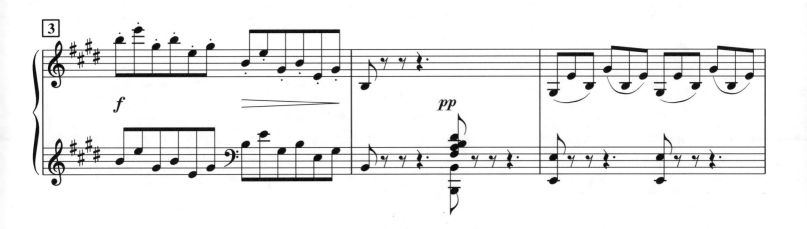

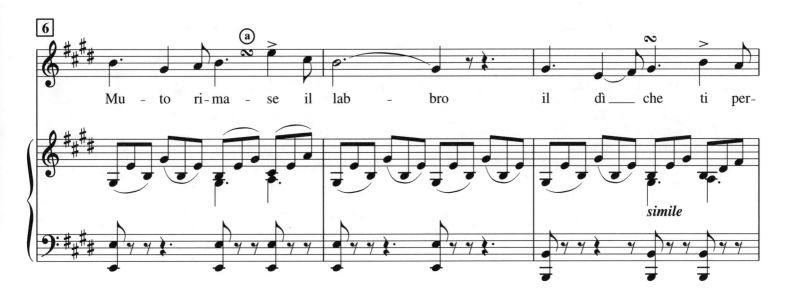

(a) To be performed:

Mu - to ri - ma - se il lab - bro   il dì __ che __ ti per-

Literal translation: I was without words the day that we parted,

⓫ The turns in measures 10 and 12, as well as all subsequent turns, are to be performed the same as those in measures 6 and 8.

ⓒ To be performed:

Spa – ri – ro i so – gni

ⓓ To be performed like measure 14.

ⓔ Sing the vowel *a* on the last note of the turn.

but my affection for you has not changed. The sweet dreams vanished; the hours during which this suffering heart thought on you seemed to be hours of torture.

ⓕ The grace notes are sung on the vowel a; time is taken from the preceding eighth note.

I tried to diminish my anguish and looked for another love, but your face was always in front of me. Ah yes, for you, my dear,

I left my native land, lit by a sorrowful sun. Perhaps if I go far enough away, my dear, I shall not suffer in this way.

4 LA STELLA

Saverio Mercadante
savɛrjo merkadante
(Altamura, 1795 - Naples, 1870)

bruno ɛ il tʃɛlo soltanto una stelːla
1 Bruno è il cielo, soltanto una stella
Dark is the sky; only one star

ɛ redʒina del vasto emisfɛro.
2 È regina del vasto emisfero.
is queen of-the vast hemisphere.

rimirandola ditʃe il pensjɛro
3 Rimirandola dice il pensiero:
Gazing-at-it says the thought:

non ɛ mia ma splɛnde per me
4 Non è mia, ma splende per me!
"Not is-it mine, but it-shines for me."

a bɛlːlastro ke puro tadʒiri
5 Ah! bell'astro, che puro t'aggiri,
Ah, beautiful-star, which, pure, moves-around-you

riskjarando la foska mia vita
6 Rischiarando la fosca mia vita,
illuminating the gloomy my life,

di tua lutʃe la dʒɔja gradita
7 Di tua luce la gioia gradita,
of your light the joy welcome,

nɔ non sia daltri ma splɛnda per me
8 No, non sia d'altri, ma splenda per me!
No, not may-it-be of-others, but may-it-shine for me!

al tuo radːʒo di vita fia doltʃe
9 Al tuo raggio di vita fia dolce
In your ray, of life may-it-be sweet

sopːportar le nɔje segrɛte
10 Sopportar le noie segrete,
to-bear the sorrows secret

ke kwel radːʒo nel kɔr ripɛte
11 Ché quel raggio nel cor ripete:
because that ray in-the heart repeats:

si son tua e risplɛndo sol per te
12 Sì, son tua, e risplendo sol per te.
Yes, I-am yours and I-shine only for you.

Background

Giuseppe Saverio Mercadante, born in a little mountain village near Bari, moved to Naples to study with the composer Nicola Zingarelli. He wrote his first opera in 1819 and he soon began a career of international popular success. In the following years he held various positions in Italy, Spain and Portugal. His works were performed in northern Europe as well, and in 1836 Rossini invited him to write an opera for the Théatre Italien in Paris.

Although many scholars have felt that Mercadante was influenced by Rossini and Bellini, in fact his musical style anticipates that of Verdi and succeeding generations. Mercadante composed over 60 operas and a vast amount of vocal chamber music that is as yet uncatalogued: songs for the drawing room, songs written on commission for music magazines, but also hundreds of re-created popular Neapolitan ballads and *canzoni.*

"*La Stella*" was printed by Pietro and Lorenzo Clausetti, one of the earliest publishing firms to set up offices in Naples, with headquarters near the San Carlo Opera. In 1864 they joined forces with Ricordi of Milan, becoming Ricordi's representatives in the south of Italy.

Mercadante probably composed "*La Stella*" in the 1850s. The text would be quite regular in form were it not for metric irregularities in the third stanza, which result from the composer's adjustments, such as adding an insignificant word or dropping an unneeded final vowel, for musical reasons.

The first stanza of the song is set in the style of an accompanied recitative, the other two stanzas forming the aria. The entire second stanza exemplifies the beautiful melodies for which Mercadante was justly famous. The word *splenda* (shine) inspires an expressive cadenza as the climax of this part. The third stanza explores the relative minor key, associated with the troubles of life. The phrase *ché quel raggio* brings back the main theme, but the continuation is altered and extended to reiterate the loving message of the final phrase. Another composer might have added an elaborate cadenza at the end, but Mercadante seems to prefer sincere simplicity: The singer holds a long, unadorned tone without accompaniment before cadencing gently and briefly.

Notable in this song is Mercadante's preference for double-dotted eighth-note rhythms, which contrast sharply with the triplets prevalent in the accompaniment.

"*La Stella*" can be sung by either a male or a female singer. The range of the song makes it ideal for any competent student or gifted amateur.

La Stella

Romanza

Saverio Mercadante

Literal translation: The sky is dark; one single star is queen of the vast heavens.

(a) "Presto" here means to play the chords promptly, without delay. This instruction does not alter the prevailing tempo.
Gazing at her, my mind says: She is not mine, but shines for me! Ah, beautiful star, the purity of your motion

brings light into my gloomy life. The joy of your light makes me happy:

it seems you are not shining for others, but for me! The rays you shed

bring sweetness, helping me bear my secret sorrows. In my heart that ray repeats: Yes, I am yours, and I shine only for you!

te,   e ri-splɛn-do per   te,   son

tu - a,   son   tu - a,   e ri - splɛn - do sol_____ per

te,   son   tu - a,   son   tu - a,   e ri -

splen - do   per   te,   per_____ te

L'ABBANDONATA (The Forsaken One)
[labːbandonˈata]

Saverio Mercadante
[savˈɛrjo merkadˈante]
(Altamura, 1795 - Naples, 1870)

lˈundʒi da te bɛn mˈio
1 Lungi da te, ben mio,
Far from you, dear mine,

per me non va ke pjˈanto
2 Per me non v'ha che pianto.
for me not there-is but weeping.

mˈuto ɛ il mˈio lˈabːbro al kˈanto
3 Muto è il mio labbro al canto,
Mute is the my lip to-the singing;

ˈoɲːɲi pjatʃˈer mˈori
4 Ogni piacer morì.
every pleasure died.

ˈai ke di nwˈɔva fjˈamːma
5 Ahi! Che di nuova fiamma
Alas, that of new flame

fˈorse tu avˈːvampi in kˈɔre
6 Forse tu avvampi in core,
perhaps you ignite in heart,

e pel novˈɛlːlo amˈore
7 E pel novello amore
and for-the new love

skˈɔrdi la tˈua fedˈel
8 Scordi la tua fedel.
you-forget the your faithful-one.

delːle mˈie pˈene atrˈotʃi
9 Delle mie pene atroci
Of-the my pains atrocious

kwˈale rakːkˈɔlsi frˈutːto
10 Quale raccolsi frutto?
what did-I-gain result?

sol di kwestˈalma il lˈutːto
11 Sol di quest'alma il lutto,
Only of this-soul the mourning,

la mˈɔrte del mˈio kˈɔr
12 La morte del mio cor.
the death of-the my heart.

non vˈɔʎːʎa idːdˈio punˈirti
13 Non voglia Iddio punirti,
Not may-wish God to-punish-you

dˈei mjˈei sofˈːfɛrti afːfˈanːni
14 Dei miei sofferti affanni;
for-the my suffered troubles

perdˈoni a te ʎˈːʎiŋganˈːni
15 Perdoni a te in ganni,
may-God-pardon to you the deceits

e me rikjˈami in tʃˈɛl
16 E me richiami in Ciel!
and me re-summon into Heaven!

Background

Please read about Mercadante on the page preceding "*La Stella.*"

In 1838 Mercadante lost the sight of one eye, making travel difficult, and he returned to Naples, where he felt at home. In 1840 he succeeded Zingarelli as director of the conservatory of Naples and held that position until his death. Even though he eventually lost the sight of the second eye, he continued to compose by dictating to his students.

"*L'Abbandonata*" is dedicated to Giuseppina Verdi (1815-1897), who was Verdi's second wife. Known during her career as Giuseppina Strepponi, she had been a very popular prima donna in the years in which Mercadante's operas were being produced in Mi-

lan and in northern Europe.

The song was published in 1869 in an *Album per canto* published by Ricordi, Milan, to raise money for the ailing poet, Francesco Maria Piave. Piave had written the librettos for Verdi's *Rigoletto, La Traviata*, and other operas. Verdi proposed the idea of the volume, which also contained works by Cagnoni, Auber, Ricci and Thomas.

The melodic line of "*L'Abbandonata*" is typically melancholic and Neapolitan, with long phrases. In these respects Mercadante's 1869 song resembles Vaccai's 1836 "*L'Addio,*" as it does in form. In both songs the first and third poetic stanzas are set to music in minor and the second and fourth in major. Vaccai's song plunges back

into minor at the end, while Mercadante's ends in major, as the abandoned woman hopes for Heaven.

Despite similarities between the two songs, their emotional impact is quite different: Vaccai's farewell is gracefully melodious, but Mercadante's dramatic outbursts require extremes of dynamics. Pianissimo is the most frequent dynamic marking in this song, and fortissimo ranks next. This is clearly the music of a theatrical composer, one who aimed not merely to please listeners but to wrench their hearts.

"*L'Abbandonata*" should be sung by a woman to a man. A male singer could adapt the text by changing "*la tua fedel*" to "*il tuo fedel.*"

L'Abbandonata
Romanza

Saverio Mercadante

Lun - gi da te, bɛn mi - o,

Per me non v'ha che pian - to, per me non v'ha che pian -

to. Mu - to è il mio lab - bro al can - to, O - gni pia -

(a) Sing the two grace notes ahead of the beat, arriving on the half-note exactly with the chord in the accompaniment.
Literal translation: Far from you, my dear, I can do nothing but cry. My lips are unable to sing, every pleasure

is dead. Woe on me! Your heart is surely burning with desire for a new love, and in your ardor

(b) Sing the ornament as an acciaccatura, as quickly as possible and ahead of the beat.

(c) Play the two grace notes ahead of the beat, just as the singer did in measure 8.

you have forgotten she who is faithful to you.

(d) Sing the two grace notes ahead of the beat, as in measure 8.

What have I gained by my atrocious sufferings? Only sorrow for my soul, and death within my heart.

I do not ask God to punish you for the suffering you have caused; may He forgive you for your deceitfulness

ⓔ Sing the acciaccatura as in measure 35.

and call me to Heaven.

OH, VIENI AL MARE (Oh, Come to the Sea!)

[o vjɛni al mɑre]

Gaetano Donizetti
[gaetano donitsetːti]
(Bergamo, 1797 - Bergamo, 1848)

vjɛni la bɑrka ɛ prɔnta
1 Vieni, la barca è pronta,
Come, the boat is ready,

ljɛve unauretːta spiɾa
2 Lieve un'auretta spira,
lightly a-little-breeze blows,

tutːto damor sospiɾa
3 Tutto d'amor sospira,
everything of-love sighs,

il mar la tɛrːra il tʃɛl
4 Il mar, la terra, il ciel.
the sea, the earth, the sky.

vedi lardʒɛntea luna
5 Vedi, l'argentea luna
See, the-silvery moon

splɛnde aʎːʎi amanti amika
6 Splende agli amanti amica,
shines to-the lovers, friend,

e sɛmbra ke ti dika
7 E sembra che ti dica:
and it-seems that to-you she-says:

korːri alːla tua fedel
8 "Corri alla tua fedel!"
Run to your faithful-one!

dɛ vjɛn gartson dʒentile
9 Deh! vien, garzon gentile,
Please, come, boy kind,

kio nel tuo sen minfɔnda
10 Ch'io nel tuo sen m'infonda,
so-that-I in your bosom may-myself-infuse,

e rasːsomiʎːʎi alːlonda
11 E rassomigli all'onda
and may-be-similar to-the-wave

ke batʃa il tʃɛlo e mwɔr
12 Che bacia il Cielo e muor.
which kisses the sky and dies.

dɛ kwanti flutːti a il mɑre
13 Deh! quanti flutti ha il mare
Please, as-many tides has the sea

io tanti batʃi avɛsːsi
14 Io tanti baci avessi;
I so-many kisses would-have;

vorːrɛi laʃːʃar kon esːsi
15 Vorrei lasciar con essi
I-would-like to-leave with them

sulːle tue labːbra il kɔr
16 Sulle tue labbra il cor.
on your lips the heart.

Background

Gaetano Donizetti learned music at an early age, thanks to a charity music school organized by the composer Simone Mayr. Through Mayr he gained early insight into the music of Haydn and Mozart. He completed his studies in Bologna with Father Stanislao Mattei, the teacher of Morlacchi and Rossini. After several years of conducting regularly and composing two to five operas a year in Naples, Donizetti achieved wider recognition with *Anna Bolena* (Milan, 1830) and other works. He traveled to Paris in 1838 upon invitation from Rossini; there he wrote operas to both French and Italian librettos. Donizetti composed over seventy operas, including several that are still performed often, such as *Lucia di Lammermoor, L'Elisir d'amore, La fille du régiment,* and *Don Pasquale.* He composed over 170 songs, of which more than 80 were printed during his lifetime. He wrote quickly and clearly, laboring incessantly throughout his professional life to fulfill the ever mounting pile of commissions.

This song is the first of ten songs and duets in a volume entitled *Matinée musicale,* dedicated to Queen Victoria of England. The album was published by Giraud, Naples, and then by Lucca, Milan, 1841/42.

Queen Victoria's diary does not mention the album, but this song would have been ideal for her voice, an agile, high soprano. She also loved Italian opera, and she had chosen arias by Donizetti to be sung in a concert honoring her 16th birthday and performed by the greatest Italian singers of the day: Malibran, Grisi, and Rubini. The song recreates a typical Neapolitan folk song, and the opening part of the melody could have been heard in any part of the city or down by the harbor. Donizetti transformed elements of popular music into a little gem for drawing room or concert hall use.

A later source calls this song "*La Gondoliera: barcarola,*" but that title implies a Venetian background and a slow, dreamy tempo, neither of which suits the song.

In measure 62, after the free cadenza, a syncopated rhythm is performed on the first syllable of *vieni.* This is called a *ribattuta di gola* (literally, restriking of the throat) and consists of underlining the vowel with a quick throb, but without stopping and restarting the tone.

Oh, vieni al mare!

Gaetano Donizetti

a Sing the two grace notes as quickly as possible and before the fifth beat of the measure, <u>or</u> sing the notes of the fourth beat as a triplet.

Literal translation: Come, the boat is ready, a little breeze is blowing, everything whispers of love, the sea, the earth, the sky!

ⓑ Sing the ornament as an acciaccatura, as quickly as possible and ahead of the beat.
Look how the silvery moon shines with pleasure on the lovers, and seems to tell you: hurry to your beloved!

© To be performed:

muɔr,____ che ____

Come to me, oh my sweet one, let me lay my head on your breast, and be like the wave that kisses the sky and then dies.

muor. Deh! quan-ti flut - ti ha il ma - re,___ io tan-ti ba - ci a-

vɛs - si;___ vor - rɛi la - sciar con es - si___

sul - le tue lab-bra il cɔr.___

Vie - ni__ la__ bar - ca ɛ̀ pron - ta,___ lie - ve u - n'au - ret - ta

I'd like to have as many kisses as the sea has floodtides. Oh that I could leave, like them, the impression of my lips on your heart!

MALVINA

Gaetano Donizetti
[gaɛtano donitsɛtːti]
(Bergamo, 1797 - Bergamo, 1848)

dal   di   ke   unaltra   ti   fu   pju   bɛlːla
1 Dal   dì   che   un'altra   ti   fu   più   bella,
Since-the   day   that   an-other   to-you   was   more   beautiful

la   vita   io   sɛnto   da   me   fudːʒir
2 La   vita   io   sento   da   me   fuggir.
the   life   I   feel   from   me   flee.

or   ke   malvina   non   ɛ   pju   kwɛlːla
3 Or   che   Malvina   non   è   più   quella,
Now   that   Malvina   not   is   anymore   that-one,

malvina   brama   solo   morir
4 Malvina   brama   solo   morir.
Malvina   desires   only   to-die.

pur   la   sua   votʃe   aŋko   timplɔra
5 Pur   la   sua   voce   anco   t'implora,
Yet   the   her   voice   again   you-implores

non   per   tʃerkarti   lantiko   amor
6 Non   per   cercarti   l'antico   amor,
not   to   seek-for-you   the-old   love

ma   per   vedɛrti   vedɛrti   aŋkora
7 Ma   per   vederti,   vederti   ancora,
but   to   see-you,   see-you   again

pria   ke   la   kɔpra   letɛrno   orːror   orːrore
8 Pria   che   la   copra   l'eterno   orror [orrore].
before   that   her   covers   the-eternal   horror.

tafːfrɛtːta   aduŋkwe   la   mɔrte   apːprɛsːsa
9 T'affretta   adunque,   la   morte   appressa:
Yourself-hurry   then,   the   death   draws-near:

vjɛni   a   vedɛre   ki   mwɔr   per   te
10 Vieni   a   vedere   chi   muor   per   te
Come   to   see   one-who   dies   for   you,

ki   per   te   mwɔre   trafitːta   e   opːprɛsːsa
11 Chi   per   te   muore,   traffitta   e   oppressa
who   for   you   dies,   wounded   and   overwhelmed

di   dwɔl   di   pjanto   damor   di   fe
12 Di   duol,   di   pianto,   d'amor,   di   fé.
of   sorrow,   of   weeping,   of love,   of   fidelity.

ma   non   lambaʃːʃa   delːlagonia
13 Ma   non   l'ambascia   dell'agonia,
But   not   the-anguish   of-the-agony,

non   delːla   mɔrte   latro   palːlor
14 Non   della   morte   l'atro   pallor,
not   of   death   the-cruel   pallor

a   te   dirانːno   kɛlːla   moria
15 A   te   diranno   ch'ella   moria
to   you   they-will-say   that-she   died

damor   di   pjanto   e   di   dolɔre
16 D'amor,   di   pianto,   e   di   dolore.
of-love,   of   weeping,   and   of   sorrow.

sol   kwando   fjɔka   zmarːrita   erːrante
17 Sol   quando   fioca,   smarrita,   errante,
Only   when   faint,   perplexed,   wandering-in-mind,

pju   lorme   tue   non   kontɛra
18 Più   l'orme   tue   non   conterà;
more   the-footsteps   your   not   she-will-expect

sol   kwando   al   radːʒo   del   tuo   sembjante
19 Sol   quando   al   raggio   del   tuo   sembiante
only   when   to-the   ray   of   your   countenance

onːɲi   sua   fibra   pju   fremera
20 Ogni   sua   fibra   più   fremerà,
every   her   fiber   more   will-thrill,

kwandil   mio   labːbro   non   pju   nomarti
21 Quand'il   mio   labbro   non   più   nomarti,
when-the   my   lip   no   more   to-name-you

ne   potra   il   tʃiʎːʎo   segwirti   aŋkora
22 Né   potrà   il   ciglio   seguirti   ancora,
nor   will-be-able   the   eye   to-follow-you   still,

kwando   il   mio   kwɔre   potra   pju   amarti
23 Quando   il   mio   cuore   potrà   più   amarti,
when   the   my   heart   will-be-able   more   to-love-you,

avrɔ   la   vita   kompita   alːlora
24 Avrò   la   vita   compita   allora.
I-shall-have   the   life   completed   then.

malvina   sol   vwɔl   vedɛrti   aŋkora
25 Malvina   sol   vuol   vederti   ancora.
Malvina   only   wants   to-see-you   again.

Background

Please read more about Donizetti in the essay that precedes *"Oh, vieni al mare!"*

In 1844, when Donizetti composed *"Malvina,"* he was living in Paris. The next year he had a heart attack and returned home to Bergamo, where he died.

This song, described as a *scena drammatica* (dramatic scene), was dedicated originally to Giovannina de Sterlich and published by Edition Schoenberger, Paris. The present edition is based on a later publication by Giraud in Naples with Italian and French texts, rededicated to the French singer Ida Bertrand, whom Donizetti must have heard and admired in Paris. She was described by the famous vocal teacher and theoretician, Heinrich Panofka, as "one of the most outstanding real deep contralto voices of her generation."

Malvina

Scena drammatica

G. Vitali

Gaetano Donizetti

Literal translation: From the day in which you loved another, my life began to cease.
Now that Malvina is no longer your favorite, Malvina

brama solo morir. Pur la sua voce anco t'im-plora, non percerti l'antico amor, ma per vederti, vederti ancora, pria che la copra l'eterno orror, pria che la copra l'eterno orrore. T'affretta a-

wishes only to die. Her voice implores you yet again, not for the return of your love, but to see you,
see you once more before she descends into eternal horror. Hurry,

her death is near; come and see her who dies for you, who dies abandoned and oppressed with sorrow, tears, and love. But when you see her anguish, see her pale complexion, you will know

that she is dying of love, tears and sorrow. Only when she is fragile, lost and wandering,
will she no longer follow your shadow, whenever

she sees your likeness she will tremble violently. When my lips no longer call your name, when my eyes see you no longer, when my heart stops loving you, then my life will have ended.

Malvina only wants to see you, to look at you once more!

AH! NON LO DIR!

Nicola de Giosa
[nikɔla dedʒoza]
(Bari, 1819–Bari, 1885)

a   non   lo   dir   bɛlːlandʒelo
1 Ah!   non   lo   dir,   bell'angelo,
Ah,   do-not   it   say,   beautiful-angel,

ke   obːbliarti   io   dɛbːba   ormai
2 Che   obbliarti   io   debba   ormai.
that   to-forget-you   I   ought   ever.

idːdio   lo   sa   non   ʎi   wɔmini
3 Iddio   lo   sa,   non   gli   uomini,
God   it   knows,   not   the   men,

se   oɲːɲora   tadorai
4 Se   ognora   t'adorai.
if   at-all-times   you-I-adored.

fosti   il   primjɛro   e   luniko
5 Fosti   il   primiero   e   l'unico
You-were   the   first   and   the-only

pensjɛr   di   kwesto   kɔre
6 Pensier   di   questo   core.
thought   of   this   heart.

potrɔ   morir   ma   spɛɲːɲere
7 Potrò   morir,   ma   spegnere
I-may   die,   but   die-out

non   mai   potrɔ   lamor
8 Non   mai   potrò   l'amor.
not   ever   may   the-love.

non   lo   dire   kio   toblii
8b (Non   lo   dire   ch'io   t'oblii,
(Not   it   say   that-I   you-should-forget,

non   mai   spɛɲːɲer   potrɔ   kwesto   amore
8c Non   mai   spegner   potrò   questo   amore.)
not   ever   die-out   may   this   love.

konfɔrta   aduŋkwe   un   mizero
9 Conforta   adunque   un   misero,
Comfort   then   a   miserable-one,

non   mi   rapir   la   spɛme
10 Non   mi   rapir   la   speme
Do-not   from-me   rob   the   hope

in   tɛrːra   tɛko   vivere
11 In   terra   teco   vivere
On   earth   with-you   to-live

o   in   tʃɛl   sarɛmo   insjɛme
12 O   in   ciel   saremo   insieme.
or   in   Heaven   we-will-be   together.

Background

Nicola de Giosa studied with Zingarelli and later with Donizetti, whose favorite pupil and protégé he became.

De Giosa was a professional conductor and composer. During his lifetime he wrote 20 operas, 400 songs, mostly *romanze*, sacred music, and enormously successful popular songs in the Neapolitan style. He is best remembered for his comic operas, written in the tradition of *opera buffa*. The most famous were *La Casa di tre artisti, Don Checco,* and *Napoli di Carnevale.* He presented his own works wherever he was invited to conduct, and in this way he introduced his operas in theaters in Italy, Egypt, and South America.

"Ah, non lo dir!" was composed to a text by Eugenia Bolmida, an amateur poet. The poem apparently consisted originally of three four-line stanzas. Extra words, unrhymed and unmetered, were added by the composer to serve his musical needs; they are set in parentheses above as in lines 8b and 8c.

This is an example of a song inspired by an advanced state of Romantic anxiety or ecstasy. The song is halfway between a popular Neapolitan ballad and a melodramatic *scena.* It develops very simply, is thoroughly melodic, and requires excellent breath control for the long phrases.

Either a man or a woman may sing this *romanza.* If a woman sings it, the words *un misero* can easily be changed to *una misera.* De Giosa's indication *con passione* means "with great feeling." When he later uses the term *mollemente,* he means "calmly, fluidly, without undue emphasis but with sentiment."

Ah! non lo dir!

Romanza

Eugenia Bolmida

Nicola de Giosa

Literal translation: Don't tell me, dear heart, that I must forget you. God knows, even if men don't, how much I still adore you.

You were my first and only thought within my heart. I shall die, but shall never cease to love you.

Bring comfort to my sorrow, don't take my hope away, that on earth I can live near you and in Heaven we'll be united.

LA VOLUBILE
[la volubile]

Nicola de Giosa
[nikɔla dedʒoza]
(Bari, 1819–Bari, 1885)

ɔ   ventanːni   son vetːsoza
1 **Ho**   **vent'anni,**   **son vezzosa,**
I-am twenty-years-old, am   pretty,

freska son komuna rɔza
2 **Fresca son com'una rosa,**
fresh   I-am as-a   rose,

kome laura delːla sera
3 **Come l'aura   della sera,**
as   the-breeze of-the evening,

kome un fjor di primavera
4 **Come un fior   di primavera.**
as   a flower of spring.

son dʒentile e a me dinːnanti
5 **Son gentile, e   a me d'innanti**
I-am nice   and to me before

milːle amanti fɔ laŋgwir
6 **Mille   amanti fo   languir!**
thousand lovers I-make languish.

se me dikon ke son belːla
7 **Se mi   dicon   che son bella,**
If to-me they-say that I-am beautiful

kome in tʃelo vaga stelːla
8 **Come in cielo vaga stella,**
as   in sky lovely star,

ke ɔ   la fatːʃa porporina
9 **Che ho   la faccia porporina,**
that I-have the face   rosy

ke ɔ   la bokːka koralːlina
10 **Che ho   la bocca corallina,**
that I-have the mouth dear-coral

del mio krin in oɲːɲi ritːʃo
11 **Del mio crin in ogni   riccio**
of my   hair in every curl

va   un kapritːʃo va   un sospir
12 **V'ha   un capriccio, v'ha   un sospir!**
there-is a   caprice,   there-is a   sigh!

tutːte larte   delːla dɔnːna
13 **Tutte l'arte   della   donna**
All   the-arts of-the woman

ma   inseɲːɲate la mia nɔnːna
14 **M'ha   insegnate la mia nonna.**
me-has taught   the my grandmother.

sɔ   dantsar sɔ   far   lokːkjetːto
15 **So   danzar, so   far   l'occhietto,**
I-know to-dance, I-know to-make the-glance

son di tutːte lidoletːto
16 **Son di tutte l'idoletto.**
I-am of all   the-dear-idol.

sɛmpre sɛmpre kanto e   rido
17 **Sempre sempre canto e   rido,**
Always, always I-sing and I-laugh,

e   konkwido oɲːɲi bɛl kɔr
18 **E   conquido ogni bel   cor.**
and I-conquer every good heart.

Background

Please read about de Giosa in the preface to "*Ah! non lo dir!*"

"*La Volubile*" was dedicated to a Miss Nathalie Hogé and published by Cottrau in Naples. This kind of song, sometimes called a *bizzaria* or musical eccentricity, was the drawing room equivalent of the comic patter song that lives on in the operettas of Arthur Sullivan and of Jacques Offenbach. Such songs have always been part of the Neapolitan tradition and must be sung very quickly and with great verve. Arias in this style are found even in the earliest Neapolitan operas and were inserted into every comic opera up to and including those of Donizetti.

This song is a real tongue twister, and great care must be taken to enunciate all the consonants clearly and cleanly. The composer added this note about the interpretation of the song:

"This scherzo should be treated with much vivaciousness and caprice. For effect, a strict tempo should not be observed in some places."

Conquido is an obsolete form of *conquisto* (I-conquer), used because of the rhyme with *rido*.

La Volubile

Scherzo

Nicola de Giosa

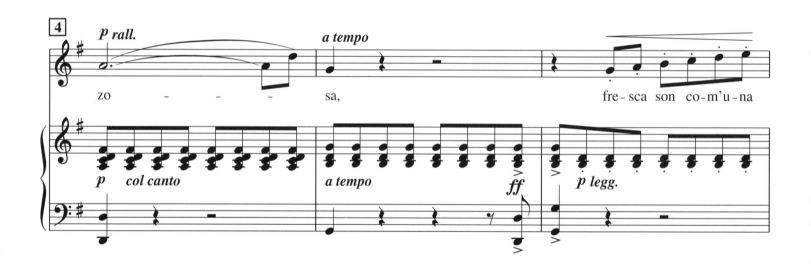

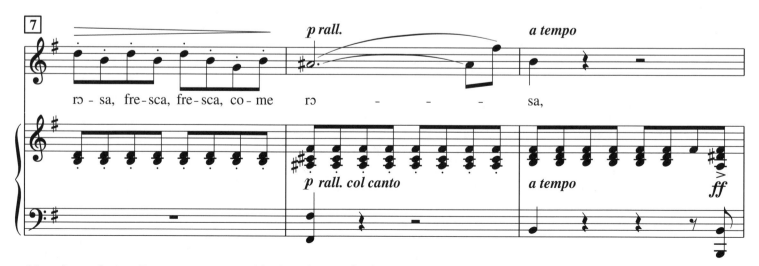

Literal translation: I am twenty years old, charming, as fresh as a rose,

like the evening breeze, like a spring flower.

I am sweet, and before me thousands of lovers languish.

They tell me that I'm as beautiful as a lovely star in the sky, that my face is rosy, that my mouth is the color of coral.

Every curl on my head is capricious. The art of being a woman

was taught me by my grandmother. I can dance, I can flirt, I'm the little idol of all. Always singing and laughing,

I conquer everyone's heart!

L'ECO (The Echo)

Amilcare Ponchielli
[amilkₐre poŋkjɛlːli]
(Paderno, 1834 - Milan, 1886)

lɛnto kavₐlka per valːli ombrₒze
1 Lento cavalca per valli ombrose
Slowly rides-a-horse through valleys shadowy

un dʒovintʃɛl
2 Un giovincel!
a youth!

vₐdo tra doltʃi bratːʃa amorₒze
3 "Vado tra dolci braccia amorose,
"Go-I toward sweet arms loving,

o vₐdo invetʃe nel kupo avɛl
4 O vado invece nel cupo avel?"
or go-I instead into-the dark tomb?"

lɛko rispₒnde nel kupo avɛl
5 L'eco risponde: "Nel cupo avel!"
The-echo answers: "Into-the dark tomb!"

il suo kamːmino segwita mₑsto
6 Il suo cammino seguita mesto
The his path continues sad

7 Il giovincel!

nelːlavɛl duŋkwe vₐdo si prₑsto
8 "Nell'avel dunque vado sì presto,
"Into-the-grave then if-go-I so early,

or bɛn ke mₒnta la patʃe ɛ in kwel
9 Or ben? Che monta? La pace è in quel!"
now good? Why ride? The peace is in that!"

10 L'eco risponde: "La pace è in quel!"

kadon dalːlɔkːkjo stilːle segrₑte
11 Cadon dall'occhio stille segrete
Fall from-the-eye tears secret

al dʒovintʒɛl
12 Al giovincel!
of-the youth.

a se il solo avɛlːlo mi da kwₑte
13 "Ah! Se il solo avello mi dà quete,
"Ah, if the only tomb me gives quiet

ljɛto vi ʃɛndo doltʃe ɛ lavɛl
14 Lieto vi scendo, dolce è l'avel!"
happy here I-dismount, sweet is the-tomb!"

lɛko ripₑte doltʃe ɛ lavɛl
15 L'eco ripete: "Dolce è l'avel!"
The-echo answers: "Sweet is the-tomb!"

Background
Amilcare Ponchielli was born near Cremona in the village of Paderno Fasolaro, now on the map as Paderno Ponchielli. He studied at the Conservatory in Milan. At age 22 he wrote an opera based on a famous novel by Manzoni, *I promessi sposi*. Revised in 1872, this opera became Ponchielli's first great success. He fell in love with his leading soprano and married her; Teresina Brambilla Ponchielli (1845-1921) became one of the most important Verdian sopranos of the century. With Verdi himself conducting, she took part in productions of *La Forza del destino, Il Trovatore* and *Aida*, and she also sang in the first Italian production of Wagner's *Lohengrin*. In 1876 Ponchielli composed for Teresina the leading role in *La Gioconda*, based on a drama by Victor Hugo and the only opera by Ponchielli that remains in today's repertory. In 1880 he began to teach at the conservatory in Milan; among his students were Puccini and, briefly, Mascagni.

Ponchielli was not prolific, but he influenced the birth of a new form of opera, *verismo*, or realism. With the end of *Il Risorgimento* and the birth of Italian nationhood, the public wanted realistic dramas that mirrored the new social order. Even though *La Gioconda* was set in 17th-century Venice, the emotions of the characters were far more credible than those of figures found in operas by Rossini, Donizetti or Bellini.

"*L'Eco*" has as its hero a singularly depressed young man. The answers that he believes he hears to his rhetorical questions are in fact his own words repeated by an echo, and these convince him that he is destined to die young. Many Italian songs of this period are about conflicting emotional feelings or impossible romantic involvements. Since an imaginary or sublimated love story rarely has anything in common with real life, most of the vocal love stories end in dreams or death.

This little song, which can be narrated by either a male or female singer, is really a series of brief musical fragments. What is of particular interest is that all three narrative episodes are sung in a minor key, but the youth's speeches and the echo's answers are in major.

"*L'Eco*" was first published posthumously.

L'Eco

Amilcare Ponchielli

Literal translation: A young man rides slowly through a shaded valley! "Shall I go towards loving arms or shall I go to a dark tomb? The echo

replies: "To a dark tomb!" The young man continues to ride, but with mounting depression! "Shall I descend to my tomb ere long, why should I ride on if my peace is therein?" The echo replies: "Peace is therein." Secret tears fall from the young man's eyes.

a Sing the ornament as an acciaccatura, as quickly as possible and ahead of the beat.

"Ah, if the tomb alone can give me peace, then I shall go willingly; sweet is the tomb!"
The echo repeated: "Sweet is the tomb!"

NON T'ACCOSTARE ALL'URNA

Carlotta Ferrari
[karlɔt:ta fer:raɾi]
(Lodi, 1837 - Bologna, 1907)

non tak:kostaɾe al:lurna
1 Non t'accostare all'urna
Not draw-near to-the-urn

ke il tʃener mio rinsɛr:ra
2 Che il cener mio rinserra;
that the ash mine locks-in;

kwesta pjetɔza tɛr:ra
3 Questa pietosa terra
this merciful earth

ɛ sakra al mio dolor
4 È sacra al mio dolor.
is sacred to my sorrow.

ɔdjo ʎi af:fan:ni twɔi
5 Odio gli affanni tuoi,
I-hate the pains yours,

rikuzo i twɔi dʒatʃinti
6 Ricuso i tuoi giacinti:
I-reject the your hyacinths.

ke dʒɔvano aʎ:ʎi estinti
7 Che giovano agli estinti
What good-are to-the deceased

due laɡrime due fjor
8 Due lagrime, due fior?
two tears, two flowers?

empja dovevi al:lora
9 Empia! dovevi allora
Cruel-woman! you-had then

pɔrgermi un fil daita
10 Porgermi un fil d'aita
to-give-me a thread of-help

kwando traea la vita
11 Quando traea la vita
when dragged the life

nel:lansja nei sospir
12 Nell'ansia, nei sospir!
in-anxiety, in sighs.

a ke dinutil pjanto
13 A che d'inutil pianto
For what with-useless weeping

as:sordi la forɛsta
14 Assordi la foresta?
do-you-disturb the forest?

rispɛt:ta unombra mɛsta
15 Rispetta un'ombra mesta,
Respect a-shade sad

e laʃ:ʃala dormir
16 E lasciala dormir!
and let-her sleep.

Background

Carlotta Ferrari, pianist, singer, poet, writer and composer, was one of the few Italian women of her time who made a name for herself as a composer of full-length operas. When she was only 20 years old Ferrari wrote her first opera, *Ugo,* and raised funds for its first production in a public theater at Lecco. She conducted the highly successful performances herself and subsequently received commissions for other operas and for a Requiem Mass with which the city of Turin commemorated the death of King Carlo Alberto in 1868.

Ferrari studied singing in Milan with Giuseppina Strepponi, who became Verdi's second wife; consequently, her songs are well written for the voice. During her lifetime they were much admired in France, especially by the composer Thomas. A contemporary critic noted that "Ferrari is lively, natural, with a remarkable talent brought to maturity as the result of her serious studies. These enable her to express beauty in everything she writes."

A person of formidable intelligence and creativity, Ferrari was one of the first Italian composers to explore the relationship between contemporary poetry and music. She published several volumes of her own poetry and prose and an auto-biography.

The text of *"Non t'accostare all'urna"* was written by Jacopo Vittorelli (1749-1835), who wrote in an "Arcadian" style similar to the poetry written during the preceding century. The poem was set to music by Schubert in 1820, while he was studying with Salieri, and by Verdi in 1838.

Ferrari's song was published with other songs in an album dedicated to Count Renato Borromeo, a Milanese patron of the arts. The voice part was printed in soprano clef, although the text takes a male point of view. If a female singer so wishes, the word *empia* (cruel woman) may be changed to *empio* (cruel man).

Observe carefully the syncopated and dramatically effective rhythm in measure 20. In measures 21-23 the first edition is unclear about the timing of the quick notes in the accompaniment: in each case the first of the 32nd notes is aligned with the second triplet note in the left hand. In this edition we align the first note of each group with the third triplet note.

Non t'accostare all'urna

Melodia

Jacopo Vittorelli

Carlotta Ferrari

Non t'ac - co-sta - re al - l'ur - na che il

ce - ner mio rin - sɛr - ra, que - sta pie-to - sa

Literal translation: Do not come near the urn that holds my ashes; this

earth is sacred to my suffering. I hate your distress, I don't want your hyacinths. Of what good to the dead are tears and a few flowers?

Shameless one! you should have given me some help when I anxiously tried to continue my life.

why do you try to deafen the forest with your useless tears? Have some respect for a poor ghost, and let it sleep in peace!

LA ZINGARA

Nicola d'Arienzo
[nikɔla darjɛntso]
(Naples, 1842 - Naples, 1915)

io sono ddzingara ɔ   bruno il vizo
1 Io sono zingara,   ho   bruno il viso,
I   am   gypsy-girl, I-have dark the face,

lo zgwardo vivido doltʃe il   sorːrizo
2 Lo sguardo vivido, dolce il   sorriso,
the glance   vivid, sweet the smile,

e ppju dun   dʒovine delːla tʃitːta
3 E più d'un   giovine della città
and more than-one youth   of-the city

vagedːʒa atːtonito la mia belta
4 Vagheggia attonito la mia beltà!
yearns-for, amazed, the my beauty!

pari alːla rondine ke korːre il mondo
5 Pari alla rondine che corre il mondo,
Like to-the swallow that roves the world,

mwɔvo linstabile   pje vagabondo
6 Muovo l'instabile pié vagabondo,
I-move the-unsettled foot vagabond,

prediko ai dʒovani fortuna e   amor
7 Predico ai giovani fortuna e   amor,
I-foretell to youths luck   and love,

ai vɛkːki stɔlidi pjanto e   dolor
8 Ai vecchi stolidi pianto e   dolor.
to old-men stolid weeping and sadness.

pju duna   vergine mi vjɛne alato
9 Più d'una   vergine mi viene alato,
More than-one virgin   to-me comes near,

sonːni a ripɛtermi damor beato
10 Sogni a ripetermi d'amor beato,
dreams to tell-me of-love happy,

ed alːla krɛdula   ne swɔi dezir
11 Ed alla credula   ne' suoi desir
and to-the credulous-one in her desires

skjudo lorakolo   delːlavːvenir
12 Schiudo l'oracolo   dell'avvenir.
I-open the-forecast of-the-future.

a dantsa fɛrvida se mabːbandono
13 A danza fervida se m'abbandono,
To dance lively if I-abandon-myself,

ledːʒɛra silfide farfalːla io sono
14 Leggera silfide, farfalla io sono.
light sylph, butterfly I am.

la vispa ddzingara amar   non sa
15 La vispa zingara   amar   non sa,
The lively gypsy   to-love not knows,

ɛbːbra di vivere in liberta
16 Ebbra di vivere in libertà!
desirous to live   in freedom!

io sono ddzingara del bruno aspɛtːto
17 Io sono zingara   del bruno aspetto,
I   am gypsy   of dark appearance,

priva di patrja   priva di tɛtːto
18 priva di patria,   priva di tetto.
without any homeland, without any roof.

la mia dovitsja ɛ il   tamburin
19 La mia dovizia è il   tamburin,
The my wealth is the tambourine,

e la letitsja il mio destin
20 E la letizia il mio destin!
and the happiness the my destiny!

Background

Nicola d'Arienzo was the nephew of a famous librettist, Marco d'Arienzo (1811-1877). The latter was a civil servant in the bureaucracy of the Kingdom of the Two Sicilies; he had a passion for the theater and wrote librettos for over thirty comic and serious operas, many of which were in the Neapolitan language. These librettos were set to music by De Giosa, Mercadante, and others. Marco d'Arienzo also wrote the text for this song.

Nicola d'Arienzo had an academic career closely tied to the conservatories in Naples. Among his students were Ruggiero Leoncavallo and Luigi Denza. He composed twelve extremely lively operas and also wrote books on music theory.

"*La Zingara*" was published in the early 1870s by the famous editor F. Lucca in Milan, and quickly became a very popular song. It is quite clearly intended to show off the virtuoso capabilities of the performer. The key is brilliance: brilliant sound, clarity of pronunciation, and vivacity. The song is written to a *bolero* rhythm and is a reminder of the Spanish domination under which the Neapolitans lived for centuries, with lasting effects on their culture and music. Many Italian composers wrote about gypsies, including Mercadante, Donizetti, and Verdi, whose *Il Trovatore* was to have been called *La Zingara*. The stereotypical gypsy was as free as the air, hence the staccatos in the vocal part; they were purveyors of mysterious information, hence the minor key; and they loved to dance. The ending of the song should make us feel as if the gypsy girl is dancing away into the night!

La Zingara
Ballata

Marco d'Arienzo

Nicola d'Arienzo

Allegretto con spirito

Io so - no __

zin - ga - ra, hɔ bru - no il vi - so, lo sguar - do

Literal translation: I'm a gypsy girl, my face is brown. I have a bright expression,

a sweet smile, and more than one of the young men in this city is dazzled by my beauty. Like the

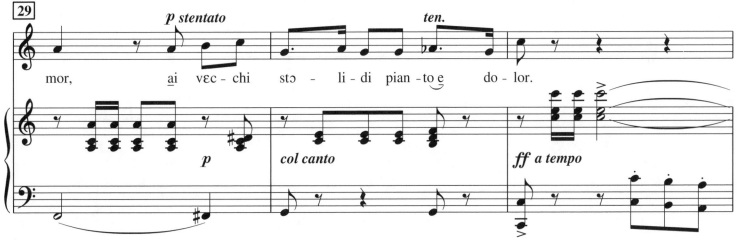

swallow that travels around the world, I am a tireless vagabond without a home. I predict fortunes and love for the young men and tears and sorrow for the stupid old ones.

Quite often young girls come to me and tell me of their dreams of love and joy, and since they want to believe what I say, I tell them what they want to hear.

(a) Sing the ornament as an acciaccatura, as quickly as possible and ahead of the third beat.

When I let myself go in frenzied dances, I'm as light as a sylph, a butterfly. But the vivacious gypsy girl can never know love; she must live and be completely free!

I am a gypsy girl with a dark face, without any homeland or any home. My wealth is my tambourine; happiness is my destiny!

stin!

a tempo

f con fuoco

Pre - di - co ai gio - va - ni for - tu - na e a - mor,

dolce stentato

ai vɛc - chi

a tempo

stɔ - li - di pian - to e do - lor, e la le -

ti - zia il mio de - stin, _____ la la, _____ la

la, _____ il mi-o de - stin, la, _____ la,

la, _____ la,

S'IO T'AMO? (Do I Love You?)

[sio tamo]

Teresa Senekè
[tereza seneke]
(Chieti, 1848 - Chieti or Rome, 1875)

kjɛder dovrɛsti alːlɛzule
1 Chieder dovresti all'esule
To-ask you-ought of-the-exile

se anɛla al swɔl natale
2 Se anela al suol natale;
if he-yearns for soil of-birth,

al fjor se spɛra unaura
3 Al fior se spera un'aura;
of-the flower if it-hopes a-breeze,

se ʎandʒeli aman dio
4 Se gl'angeli aman Dio:
if the-angels love God,

ma non dovrɛsti kjɛdermi
5 Ma non dovresti chiedermi
but not you-ought to-ask-me

sardo per te damore
6 S'ardo per te d'amore.
if-I-burn for you with-love.

mel dɛvi in fronte lɛdːʒere
7 Mel devi in fronte leggere,
Of-me-it you-should on face read,

se non mel pwɔi nel kɔr
8 Se non mel puoi nel cor.
if not of-me-it you-can in-the heart.

un gwardo sol konfondere
9 Un guardo sol confondere
One glance alone mingle

due vite pwɔ e due kɔr
10 Due vite può e due cor;
two lives can and two hearts;

pwɔ fartʃi egwali aʎːʎi andʒeli
11 Può farci eguali agli angeli
can make-us equals to-the angels

un batʃo sol damor
12 Un bacio sol d'amor.
a kiss alone of-love.

ama la tɛrːra ɛ un cartʃere
13 Ama! La terra è un carcere
Love! The earth is a prison

se non lirːradja amore
14 Se non l'irradia amore.
if not it-illuminates love.

ama la vita ɛ stratsjo
15 Ama! La vita è strazio
Love! The life is torture

a ki non arde in kɔre
16 A chi non arde in core.
to one-who not burns in heart.

se dio ti djɛde unanima
17 Se Dio ti diede un'anima,
If God to-you gave a-soul,

se un kɔr ti djɛde idːdio
18 Se un cor ti diede Iddio,
if a heart to-you gave God,

vɔlːle kalmar ʎi spazimi
19 Volle calmar gli spasimi
He-wanted to-calm the agonies

delːlalma e del kɔr mio
20 Dell'alma e del cor mio.
of-the-soul and of-the heart mine.

Background

La Palestra Musicale was a music magazine that was published seven times a year from 1866 to 1872 by Moreo of Milan. In 1871 the publishers decided to include short musical works in the magazine and to publish the same works simultaneously as separate numbers. Some music lovers collected the pieces and had them bound into volumes. The song that was chosen to inaugurate the new series on February 1, 1871, was *"S'io t'amo?"* by Teresa Senekè. The reason for this choice was that Senekè had composed an extremely successful opera, *Le due amiche*

(The Two Girlfriends), produced in Rome in 1869. Little is known about Senekè's life, except that she was born in Chieti in Tuscany; her name suggests that her family was Jewish. During her short life she composed works for voice, piano, and instrumental ensembles.

From 1625, the year in which Francesca Caccini (1587-ca.1640) produced her first opera, *La Liberazione di Ruggiero dall'Isola d'Alcina*, until the present day, nearly 200 full-length operas composed by Italian women have been produced in Italian and European opera houses. Social conditions have made it almost impossible for an

Italian woman to make herself known only as a composer, and most of the composers of these operas were first and foremost prominent performing artists. Women did, however, write and perform an enormous quantity of chamber music, songs, and piano pieces. The quality of these works differs in no way from those written by their male contemporaries, and some of the songs became "best sellers."

"S'io t'amo?" was dedicated to Donna Adele, Duchess of Castiglione Colonna, one of many Roman aristocrats who held regular musical soirées in their palaces in Rome.

S'io t'amo?
Romanza

Cantabile

Teresa Senekè

ⓐSing the ornament as an acciaccatura, as quickly as possible and ahead of the fourth beat.

Literal translation: Ask the exile if he longs for his homeland, the flower if she hopes for a breeze, if the angels love God,
but you shouldn't ask me

if I burn with love for you; you can read it on my face if you can't read it in my heart. One look can change two lives and two hearts; a single kiss renders us equal to the angels.

ⓑ Sing the ornament as an acciaccatura, as quickly as possible and ahead of the third beat.

Love! This life is a prison without love. Love! Life is a torment for those who have no love.

If God gave you a soul, if he gave you a heart, these were to calm the fear in my soul and in my heart. One look can change two lives and two hearts;

a single kiss renders us equal to the angels.

LA PESCATRICE

Alfredo Catalani
[alfredo katalani]
(Lucca, 1854 - Milan, 1893)

o dʒovanetːta peskatritʃe bɛlːla
1 **O giovanetta pescatrice bella,**
O dear-young fisher-woman beautiful,

gwida il kanotːto a prɔra e vjɛni kwa
2 **Guida il canotto a prora e vieni qua:**
steer the little-boat at prow and come here;

a me vjɛni tasːsidi e mi favɛlːla
3 **A me vieni, t'assidi e mi favella,**
to me come, yourself-seat and to-me talk,

e la tua man mi da
4 **E la tua man mi dà.**
and the your hand to-me give.

mɛtːtimi kwi sul kɔre la testina
5 **Mettimi qui sul core la testina,**
Put-me here on-the heart the little-head,

la mia bambina e tanto non tremar
6 **La mia bambina, e tanto non tremar;**
the my baby-girl, and too-much do-not tremble.

non tafːfidi sekura oɲːɲi matːtina
7 **Non t'affidi secura ogni mattina**
Don't you-trust-yourself, safe, every morning

al maɾe alːlaspro mar
8 **Al mare, all'aspro mar?**
to-the sea, to-the-rough sea?

aŋke il mio kɔre ɛ un mar a le sue ɔnde
9 **Anche il mio core è un mar, ha le sue onde,**
Also the my heart is a sea, has the its waves;

le sue tempɛste le sue ɔnde eʎːʎi a
10 **Le sue tempeste, le sue onde egli ha,**
the its tempests, the its waves it has.

e mɔlte bɛlːle pɛrle aŋke naskɔnde
11 **E molte belle perle anche nasconde**
And many beautiful pearls also hides

la sua profonditа
12 **La sua profondità.**
the its depth.

Background

The text of this song is a re-creation in Italian of a poem by Heinrich Heine (1797-1856). The intensity, brevity, and wit of Heine's poems attracted many composers from Schubert to Strauss, and this particular text was set to music by Schubert in *Schwanengesang*, published posthumously. It is highly probable that Catalani first read the poem in German and made his own translation.

This is the original:
Du schönes Fischermädchen,
Treibe den Kahn ans Land;
Komm zu mir und setze dich nieder,
Wir kosen Hand in Hand.

Leg an mein Herz dein Köpfchen
Und fürchte dich nicht so sehr;
Vertraust du dich doch sorglos
Täglich dem wilden Meer!

Mein Herz gleicht ganz dem Meere,
Hat Sturm und Ebb' und Flut,
Und manche schöne Perle
In seiner Tiefe ruht.

The following is an English translation of the German, so that one can see the small differences introduced into the Italian version.
    You lovely fisher girl,
    steer your boat to the shore;
    come to me and sit down,
    we will fondle hand in hand.

    Lay your little head on my heart
    and be not too much afraid;
    you entrust yourself fearlessly
    every day to the wild sea!

    My heart is just like the sea,
    has storm and ebb and flow,
    and many a lovely pearl
    rests in its depths.

Alfredo Catalani learned music from his father and an uncle before entering the Milan Conservatory in 1873. He remained in Milan for the rest of his life, teaching composition at the conservatory and writing operas, some symphonic works, and chamber music. His style is different from that of his contemporaries and yet was not influenced by foreign models. He wrote two operas that are still admired by connoisseurs, *Loreley* (1888) and *La Wally* (1892).

Catalani wrote only 17 songs for voice and piano of which the last was *La Pescatrice*. It was published by Ricordi and deposited with the prefect of Milan to protect the copyright on May 20, 1893, less than three months before Catalani died.

Using the rhythm of a barcarolle, Catalani has woven a subtle and colorful musical fabric in which the melodic line passes back and forth freely between voice and piano. This sophisticated manner of composition is familiar to us in the operas of Puccini, who also in 1893 brought out the earliest of his great operas, *Manon Lescaut*, which was soon to be followed by other popular masterpieces.

La Pescatrice

Lirica vocale

Heinrich Heine

Alfredo Catalani

O gio - va - net - ta pe - sca - tri - ce, pe - sca - tri - ce

bel - la,__ Gui - da il ca - not - to a pro - ra e viε - ni qua:____

Literal translation: Lovely fisher girl, let your boat glide to the shore.

Come and sit by my side, and hand in hand we will whisper together.
Lay your head on my heart and be not too afraid.

Fearlessly you entrust yourself to the wild sea every day. My heart is just like the sea: it has its waves,

Lyrics under the music:

46 Le su - e tem - pɛ - ste, le su - e on - de e - gli

49 ha, _____ E mol - te bɛl - le pɛr - le,

52 an - che na - scon - de la su - a pro - fon - di - tà. _____

riten. ⓐ

riten. col canto

a tempo

p

56

ⓐ Sing the two grace notes before the beat, but calmly.

its storms, its flood. And many a lovely pearl rests in its depths.

ITALIAN MUSICAL VOCABULARY

a piacere.........................at your pleasure, freely, not hurried

a piena voce.....................................with full voice

affrettato...hurrying

agitato..restless

allegretto..lively

allegretto con spirito.................lively, with a sense of humor

allegretto vivace...................................lively, vivacious

allegro mosso assai............................lively and fairly quickly

andante...evenly, not too quickly

andante appassionato.................................evenly, with ardor

andante mosso...........................evenly, with some movement

andantino grazioso.................at a moderate, graceful tempo

animando un poco........a little faster, with more expression

calando......................................decreasing in tone and speed

calando sempre più.............................ever softer and slower

cantabile.................................sing through the phrase evenly

cantando..in a singing way

col canto...not in strict meter

con abbandono..........................with unrestrained emotion

con accento..with emphasis

con anima...................................with transport, great feeling

con civetteria..flirting

con dolore...sorrowfully

con dolorosa espressione..............with sorrowful expression

con forza...with strength

con fuoco...with great enthusiasm

con grazia..delicately

con passione...with passion

con saddisfazione...with satisfaction

con semplicità.....................................without accents, simply

crescendo......................................gradually increasing in tone

crescendo d'entusiasmo...............with increasing enthusiasm

cupo...darkly

delicatamente...delicately

dolce stentato............................sweetly, but with emphasis

dolcissimo...sweetly

incalzando...more quickly

larghetto..fairly slowly

lento...slowly

meno mosso..less quickly

moderato assai................................fairly moderately

mollemente.................languidly, calmly, fluidly, with feeling

morendo...dying away

più animato..more lively

più sentito...................................with rather more feeling

poco agitato......................................slightly restless

portando la voce......................literally, "carrying the voice,"
but in this context the phrase
means moving smoothly
from one note to another.

quasi parlato.....................................almost spoken

rallentando....................................slowing down progressively

ridendo maliziosamente..................laughing mischievously

rinforzando.................................giving more sound

risoluto...firmly, decisively

ritenuto...............................held back in tempo, slower

scherzando..playfully

secondando...accompanying

sempre...always, continually

slanciato...rushed

slentando...slowing down

smorzando..dying away

sotto voce...whispering

stentato..emphasized

strappate..snatched, played suddenly

straziante..anguished

ten., tenuto.....................................held (less than a fermata)

trattenuto..held back

tutta forza......................................with full strength

tutta gioia...joyfully

un poco più.......................................a little faster

voce languente...with plaintive voice

LIST OF WORKS CONSULTED

Albarosa, N. *Amilcare Ponchielli: saggi e ricerche nel 150° anniversario della nascita.* Cremona, 1984.

Ashbrook, W. *Donizetti.* London, 1965.

Adkins Chiti, P. *Almanacco delle virtuose, primedonne, compositrici e musiciste d'Italia dall'A.D. 177 ai giorni nostri.* Novara, 1991.

Adkins Chiti, P. *Una voce poco fa... ovvero le musiche delle primedonne rossiniane.* Rome, 1992.

Battaile, C.A. *De l'enseignement du chant.* Paris, 1861.

Castiglione, E. *Rossini: lettere.* Rome, 1992.

Cottrau, G. *Lettres d'un mélomane.* Naples, 1885.

De Angelis, A. *La musica a Roma nel secolo XIX.* Rome, 1935.

Della Corte, A. *L'interpretazione musicale.* Rome, 1960.

Dizionario di Musica e Musicisti. Turin:UTET, 1984.

Einstein, A. *Music in the Romantic Era.* New York, 1947.

Fasano, R. *Storia degli abbellimenti.* Rome, 1957.

Florimo, F. *Breve metodo di canto.* Naples, 1870.

Florimo, F. *Cenno storico sulla scuola musicale di Napoli.* Naples, 1869-71.

Garcia, M. *Hints on Singing.* London, 1894.

Giraldoni, L. *Guida teorica e pratica dell'artista cantante.* Milan, 1864.

Lichtenthal, P. *Dizionario e bibliografia della musica.* Milan, 1826.

Maragliano Mori, R. *Coscienza della voce.* Milan, 1970.

Neri, A. *Degli abbellimenti.* Padua, 1922.

New Oxford Dictionary of Music, Vol. IX, *Romanticism.* London, 1984.

Panofka, H. *L'arte di canto.* Paris, 1866.

Panofka, H. *Voci e cantanti.* Paris, 1866.

Pellegrini Celone, M. *Grammatica, ossia regole per ben cantare.* Rome, 1817.

Radiciotti, G. *Rossini.* Tivoli, 1929.

Ricci, V. *"V.P. Tosti e la lirica vocale italiana nell'ottocento." Rivista musicale italiana,* 1917.

Romagnesi, H. *L'art de chanter les romances et généralement toute la musique de salon.* Paris, 1846.

Serafin, T., and **A. Toni.** *Stile, tradizioni e convenzioni del melodramma italiano.* Milan, 1958.

Società Italiana Autori ed Editori. *La musica colta e musica popolare.* Varazze, 1991. (Papers of the congress organized by the S.I.A.E.)

ABOUT THE AUTHOR

Patricia Adkins Chiti, dramatic mezzo-soprano, is internationally recognized for her performances in the opera house, with symphony orchestras, and on the concert stage. Born in England and trained in England, Italy and Germany, she made her operatic debut in Menotti's *Help, Help, the Globolinks!* at Rome's Teatro dell'Opera in 1972. In the same season she also made a debut as Azucena in Verdi's *Il Trovatore* at the Teatro Comunale, Bologna. She has recorded over 400 works, both for radio and for commercial release. Her recording of Shostakovich's *Six Lyrics of Marina Svetayova*, Opus 143, with the Radio Symphony Orchestra of Brussels conducted by Alfred Walter, has received great critical acclaim both in Europe and in the United States. Adkins Chiti has sung as concert soloist with many major orchestras under such conductors as Michel Tabachnik, Mstislav Rostropovich, Yehudi Menuhin, Vladimir Fedoseev, Richard Pittman and Giampiero Taverna. She has also sung first performances of many important contemporary works, including those by Sofia Gubaidulina. Her repertoire ranges from Italian, French and German opera to the nineteenth-century symphonic repertoire to music of the twentieth century.

Adkins Chiti has carried out musicological research since her student days at the Guildhall School of Music and Drama, London. Other books she has written are: *Donne in Musica* (Rome: Bulzoni, 1982; also to appear soon in a Spanish language version); *Almanack of the Virtuosas, Primadonnas, Women Composers and Musicians of Italy from 177 A.D. till the Present Day* (Novara: De Agostini, 1991); and *Una Voce Poco Fa . . . , ovvero le musiche delle primedonne rossiniane* (Rome: Garamond Editrice, 1992). She has also contributed to *The Musical Woman* (New York, 1984), *The Encyclopedia of Women Composers* (New York, 1981 and 1986), and *The Violin-Keyboard Sonata Encyclopedia* (Arkansas, 1984). In addition to essays and articles published throughout Europe, Adkins Chiti contributes regularly to the Italian newspaper *Il Giornale*. She is a well-known radio and television personality in Italy.

Patricia Adkins Chiti is married to composer Gian Paolo Chiti and, when not on her travels, lives in Rome.

The following artists are featured on the recordings that accompany this book.

Francesco Russo

Maestro Russo has been principal accompanist for Rome's famous Santa Cecilia Conservatory since 1978. He originally studied piano at the Tartini Conservatory in Trieste and subsequently studied composition with Giulio Viozzi. The versatile pianist began his career working both in the classical field and with popular music orchestras and big bands. In 1955 he was conductor of the German RIAS radio orchestra and later worked with the orchestras of the RAI (Italian radio and television network) in Trieste, Milan, Turin and Rome both as conductor and pianist. His experience and background represent a wide repertoire ranging from 15th-century music to the music of today.

Anna Teresa Eugeni

Ms. Eugeni, an Italian actress and stage director, is well known in Italy for her beautiful voice. She has dubbed the voices of many famous actresses for cinema and television, including Maureen O'Hara, Lana Turner, Yvonne de Carlo, Brigitte Bardot, Julie Christie, Liza Minnelli, Loretta Swift, Shirley MacLaine and Jane Fonda. She supervised all translations and dubbing for a televised Shakespeare series, and has also acted as artistic consultant to many Italian festivals. Her experience as a director includes work in theater, opera and television commercials.

KEY TO THE INTERNATIONAL PHONETIC ALPHABET FOR ITALIAN

Vowels

A	[a],	bright, smiling "ah," as in	*cara* [ka̠ra], *andante* [anda̠nte]
E	[e],	"closed," as in	*che* [ke], *legato* [lega̠to]
	[ɛ],	"open," as in	*ecco* [ɛ̠k:ko], *presto* [prɛ̠sto]
I	[i],	as in	*mio* [mi̠o], *divino* [divi̠no]
O	[o],	"closed," as in	*solo* [so̠lo], *così* [kosi̠]
	[ɔ],	"open," as in	*opera* [ɔ̠pera], *forte* [fɔ̠rte]
U	[u],	as in	*bruno* [bru̠no], *tuba* [tu̠ba]

(Italian spelling does not show when e̠ and o̠ are pronounced closed and when they are open. For your convenience this book shows the open e̠'s and o̠'s with IPA symbols inserted into the Italian words.)

Semi-Vowels

I	[j],	before another vowel, as in	*più* [pju], *piano* [pja̠no]
U	[w],	before another vowel, as in	*uomo* [wo̠mo], *acqua* [a̠k:kwa]

Consonants

B, F, M, and V are pronounced as in English.

D, N, T, and L are pronounced as in English, but with the tongue contacting the upper teeth.

C	[tʃ],	before e̠ or i, as in	*cielo* [tʃɛ̠lo], *cello* [tʃɛ̠l:lo]
C	[k],	otherwise, as in	*orchestra* [orkɛ̠stra], *cantata* [kanta̠ta]
SC	[ʃ],	before e̠ or i, as in	*scena* [ʃɛ̠na], *crescendo* [kreʃɛ̠ndo]
SC	[sk],	as in	*scala* [ska̠la], *scherzo* [skɛ̠rtso]
G	[dʒ],	before e̠ or i, as in	*gentile* [dʒenti̠le], *regina* [redʒi̠na]
G	[g],	otherwise, as in	*grande* [gra̠nde], *largo* [la̠rgo]
N	[ŋ],	before [k] or [g], as in	*ancora* [aŋko̠ra], *languire* [laŋgwi̠re]
QU	[kw],	as in	*quasi* [kwa̠zi], *quartetto* [kwartɛ̠t:to]
R	[ɾ],	flipped between two vowels, as in	*furore* [fuɾo̠re], *cara* [ka̠ɾa]
R	[r],	trilled in all other cases, as in	*ritardo* [rita̠rdo], *cor* [kɔr]
S	[s],	as in	*secco* [sɛ̠k:ko], *sostenuto* [sostenu̠to]
S	[z],	in some words, as in	*deciso* [detʃi̠zo], *slancio* [zlantʃo]
Z	[ts],	as in	*terzetto* [tertsɛ̠t:to], *grazia* [gra̠t:tsja]
Z	[dz],	in some words, as in	*mezzo* [mɛ̠d:dzo]

Gliding Consonants (not found in English)

GLI	[ʎ],	like [lj] but made with the middle of the tongue, as in	*scoglio* [skɔ̠ʎ:ʎo], *taglia* [ta̠ʎ:ʎa]
GN	[ɲ],	like [nj] but made with the middle of the tongue, as in	*ogni* [o̠ɲ:ɲi], *segno* [sɛ̠ɲ:ɲo]

Silent Letters

H is always silent, as in	*hanno* [a̠n:no], *honestà* [onesta̠]
H hardens C, G, and SC, as in	*chi* [ki], *meschino* [meski̠no]
I is silent when used to soften C, G, or SC, as in	*già* [dʒa], *lascia* [la̠ʃ:ʃa]

Please note: Phonetic symbols show the similarities that exist between the sounds of different languages. Nevertheless, they have slightly different values in different languages, and phonetic transcriptions can be only approximate. One still needs to listen to the way the language is sung by native Italians. Furthermore, many singers employ vowel modification, and phonetic transcriptions do not show this. The vowel pronunciations given in this book come from Zingarelli's *Vocabolario della lingua italiana*; they may be modified to accommodate your voice.